Memoirs

of a

Medium

Guisela Montes

Llumina
Press

ISBN: 978-1-62550-447-0 (PB)

Acknowledgments

I want to tell my daughter, Paola, thank you for all her hard work, dedication, and patience. Without you, this book I dreamed of would not have been possible. You are my only daughter and my strength; since the day you were born you've made me happy and proud. Thank you for your love.

I also want to dedicate this book to my husband, Paul, and my two boys, Anthony and Christopher. You are my inspiration; you all make me believe that everything is possible when love is involved.

I'd like to thank my mom, Betty, who is my hero, as well as my grandmother Isabel. Everything I am now is because of both of you. You've made me strong and able to believe in myself. Thank you for your help in every day of my life. I am lucky to have both of you watching over me in heaven. I am so lucky to have God, my angels, and my spiritual guides working side by side with me.

To my terrific brother, Luis; my sister-in-law Esperanza; my sister and best friend, Elizabeth; my lovely mother-in-law and second mom, Betty; her husband, Guy; my Dad Julio, and my wonderful sister-in-law Denise. Thank you for believing in me, for listening to my stories, and for your trust and support.

I'd also like to acknowledge my friends for their support and for believing in me. These wonderful people include Steve and Gina Parsloe, Christine Cusimano, Sharez Floyd, Jennifer Rivadeneyra, Michael and Lori Gauser, Janet Haugh, Gustavo Munoz, Marco Larrain, Diane Sanfilippo, Mauricio Belanic, Lorraine Ryan, Kathy Udell, Lillian Vignieri, Debbie Gnegy, Lorri Acott-Fowler, and anyone else whom I may have omitted. I keep you all in my heart. You are all the greatest friends anyone could ever have.

With all my love,
Guisela Montes

Table of Contents

Memoirs

of a

Medium

For Mom, from Paola

What can I say about having a mom who talks to the dead? I guess now that I think about it, there's a lot. Growing up with the dead certainly changed my life in many ways. Most of all, I can appreciate being surrounded by the spiritual realm because it gives me a glimpse into the afterlife and lets me know that there is someone out there who watches over us. If it weren't for my mother, I don't think I would have as strong a faith in God as I do today. My mom is indubitable proof to me that God exists. She is the one that teaches me that there are little miracles in everyday life.

It is because of her that I know that everything, whether good or bad, happens for a reason. She gives me hope and happiness in my life. For me, though, I grew up with a normal mom. ,Accepting the knowledge that there are things that we sometimes don't understand is a part of my everyday life. I'm glad that I was chosen to live life with a family that has these gifts. It has made me the person I am today. It has helped me understand always looking at everything with an open mind.

I am always so proud of my mom. I don't think I tell her that enough. I have always strived to be like her—strong and intelligent—and I hope that someday I can get the respect that she commands. I think that my mom is the bravest woman on earth. I have watched my mom overcome even the toughest of obstacles. When my parents separated, it was a difficult time for all of us. My mom was constantly at work, and she was also going to school while trying to raise her two kids. I did my best to help out around the house, and I learned then how to take care of others. I followed my mother's example: if she was going to work hard, I was going to work hard too. I guess you could say my mom is my prime example of what I think a woman should be. She is always putting the well-being of others before her own.

Because I am her daughter, I too can always see and hear spirits. Anytime I feel afraid, I always have my mom there to reassure me. I have seen my mom grow, and I have seen her learn how to harness her power. I am so glad that now she has such a strong connection and understanding of her gift, because she can do so much with it. All that my mom has ever done is help people that needed help, living or dead. She is caring and understanding and always wants to do good. I never doubt that God put my mother here on this earth to help people who need it.

There have been many times when I have experienced things with the other side, and I have several stories to tell, but this book is about my wonderful mom, so I think that I will stop here. There are just so many things that I could say about my mom because she does so much for us.

Mom, I love you and am so proud of you.

Kathy's Story

My first meeting with Guisela was in May 2007 when she came into my office for a sick visit. The previous six months of my life had been a whirlwind of experiences. I had gone into the operating room in November 2006 for a routine surgery, and I came out a cancer survivor. Two weeks after that, I purchased a home that my sister and I moved into. She had been diagnosed with Lou Gehrig's disease five months earlier and was now confined to a wheelchair. She was no longer able to live alone, and I became her caretaker and constant companion. The house I bought was only a mile or so from my job, and Hope Hospice House was between them both. I knew that someday we might need their services, and being close to them was reassuring.

My sister and I were a year apart, she being the younger. We had shared a troubled childhood together and survived. We were determined to make the best of whatever time either one of us had left in this lifetime. We made a pact that whoever passed first would return and let the other know that all was as we expected it to be "over there"—beautiful, loving, and amazing. I had told her she had better not come to freak me out in the middle of the night, and we both laughed. Little did we know that in two months she would be "over there."

Guisela arrived in my office and sat down on the exam table. Before I could ask her what symptoms she was having, she said, "I know your sister has passed." I thought that was odd. I couldn't imagine how she could've gotten this personal information. She then asked me if I believed in "psychic and spiritual readings." I answered yes, as I had studied under a great teacher in this exact subject in the past. Guisela then said, "Your sister asked me to come up here today and try to answer some of the questions that you have been asking her." I started to cry tears of overwhelming joy and compassion as she proceeded to tell me that my sister's legs did not hurt anymore. She mentioned some rocks that I had just purchased the day before, small river rocks with sayings on them. She talked about my sister's little dog, how my sister wanted me to get on with living, the broom I was using to sweep the porch, and the tinkling of the wind chimes when there wasn't any wind. A man had met my sister when she arrived "over there," and they would be celebrating something in July. It must've been my brother, who had passed in a plane crash seventeen years before. His birthday was in July. But the most amazing thing Guisela said was that my sister wanted me to know that every second of every minute of every hour of every day that she lived with me, she had lived to the fullest because of me. Then my sister said she couldn't stay long because there was so much happening and she didn't want to miss anything.

Since then I have had another reading with Guisela, just as amazing as the first, and I have had her give a phone reading to my sister's daughter, who was struggling with her mom's passing. The transformation in my niece since then has been remarkable. As a health care provider, I share Guisela's phone number with those who have had loved ones pass. The stories of miracles and healing that I hear back from these patients is truly beyond words. The talents that she possesses in this realm are amazing. I have had many readings with other talented souls, but Guisela truly surpasses the others. Her kindness, compassion, and diligence are evident in every encounter I have had with her.

How absolutely awesome to have people like this on our physical plane who can pick up where traditional medicine and psychology leave off and help others heal. For me, I know without a shadow of a doubt that we just change energy forms when we cease to breathe and that we continue to live in an incredible place that words cannot describe— they would only cheapen the experience.

Coincidence is God's way of remaining anonymous.

Life is God's gift to us; what we do with it is our gift to God.

May you recognize your coincidences for what they really are.

Kathy Udell

Lori's Story

When I first heard about Guisela Montes, it was through a phone call from Amy, a friend who had lost her brother to a terrible homicide about twelve years earlier. Amy and her family had not been the same since the tragic loss of her brother. She and her mother where just leaving Guisela's home after their reading, and she was eager to call me. Amy knew that I had lost my mother only about six months earlier, after her long battle with breast cancer. Now, Amy sounded happy and even excited. She had been skeptical going in but finished with no doubt that she had just had a long-awaited meeting with the brother that she never got to say goodbye to. She was eager for me to meet Guisela as well.

I understand the skeptics out there, and I know there will always be skeptics. I do not tell my experience in an effort to sway anyone or change their beliefs. I just want to share my thoughts and feelings on my own personal experience of what Guisela was able to do for me. I just ask that you try to keep an open mind.

7

My mother and I had a special mother-daughter relation-ship. We shared everything with one another, and we talked at least ten times a day, just to check on one another. My mom was the first person I spoke to in the morning and the last person I spoke to at night. My mother was sick for about ten years before passing away at a hospice in November 2007. I thought I would never survive life without her in it. But as anyone who has suffered the loss of the person who means the most to us knows, the person we've lost would not want us to suffer in sadness all the time but to find it within ourselves to live our lives the best we can. Because they are still with us, we should continue to talk to them, always acknowledge their spirit, and know we will see them again.

I went to Guisela's home with a combination of nerves, anxiety, hope, and skepticism. I took my best friend of twenty-two years along with me. She was extremely close to my mom and even called her "Mom." Guisela knew only my first name; she had no other information about me. We began the reading, and I said nothing, mostly because I was nervous but partly because everyone says "don't give any-thing away." One of the first things Guisela said to me was, "This is your mother." Guisela went on to tell me things she really could not have known: things my mom liked or said and events that had happened in my life and my siblings' lives since she had passed. She knew what kind of relation-ship my mom had had with her mom, my grandmother, and that's not an easy one to figure out. She knew that I had a picture of my mother next to my bed at home and that I had a cross dangling on the frame of the picture. She even mentioned what I made myself to eat in my kitchen most nights. This was to validate that my mother is with me and watching over me. The surprise at the reading was when Guisela mentioned someone else to me. I had a close friend pass away from leukemia in 2005. My mom also knew him and would joke during her time in hospice that she'd be playing cards up in heaven with Andy sometime soon. I honestly was so interested in hearing from my mom that I never thought Andy would show up, but he did. Guisela asked me, "Do you know a guy who's kind of feminine that's passed?" This is so funny because Andy was frequently described as feminine for a straight guy. Guisela went on to say that Andy was with my mom "playing cards," and he wanted me to know he's there too taking care of her.

My experience left me with a peaceful and calm feeling. My mother and I shared such a bond that I could already feel that she was out of pain following her passing, but Guisela confirmed it for me. She also confirmed that my mother really does still see happenings in our lives, even if she is not here in her physical form anymore. Anyone who is a decent judge of character upon meeting another person would agree after meeting Guisela that you can tell she is a warm and kind person with good intentions. She has a gift, and she truly wants to help people. Guisela has a good heart and is without alterior motives. I am not naive, and I say how I feel. I understand the skeptics' way of thinking, and I too have witnessed the guests on TV talk shows and so on who are obviously taking advantage of vulnerable people. Not all, but some. Guisela is absolutely not one of those manipulative people. A meeting with Guisela is a positive experience. She is insightful, knowledgeable, and a decent human being.

Lori Reale ☺

Our Visit with Guisela

Our father, Maurice (Murray) Joseph Wasser, first became ill in February 2007, when he was admitted to HealthPark Medical Center in Fort Myers, Florida, with a diagnosis of pneumonia. Little did we know that it was congestive heart failure and that only two months later, on April 17, his life's journey would end. We thought we would never be able to speak to him or hear from him again. That, however, changed when we met Guisela Montes, who gave us the gift of communication.

Wanting to communicate with Dad on his birthday—our first without him, on January 19, 2008—we contacted Guisela who, like Sandi, was employed at Lee Memorial Health System in Fort Myers, Florida. Having gotten her telephone number from another employee, Kathy Udell, the appointment was made, and we met at Guisela's home. It was an incredible experience!

We arrived to find her kitchen table lit with beautiful candles—and set with a glass of orange juice, which sent a strong signal to us that Dad was indeed there. Having been diagnosed with adult-onset diabetes years earlier, Dad would awake every morning hypoglycemic. As a nurse, Sandi suggested that Dad keep a thermos of orange juice on his nightstand. When getting up during the night, he would take a few sips, which helped him avoid that low blood sugar feeling in the morning. When we sat down, Guisela asked, "What is with the orange juice? Your father came to me this morning and told me to put orange juice on the table so his girls would know." We told her about the juice, and again we knew Dad was with us.

Many things said to us that afternoon reinforced our belief that Dad was definitely communicating with us through Guisela. These two, however, were the most definitive. When Sandi graduated from Florida Gulf Coast University in Fort Myers on December 15, 2007, she received a gift from a dear friend: a restored picture of Dad taken in the 1940s. Sandi kept it on a coffee table in her home, but whenever she and her fiancé would go out on the weekend, she would move the picture to a higher place so that her dog would not knock it over with his tail. During the visit with Dad, Guisela said, "Your father wants to know why you keep moving his picture." Terri responded, "I don't move Daddy's picture." But Sandi realized, "Oh my gosh, we move it every time we go out to dinner!" Since then, a permanent place has been found for Dad's picture so it no longer gets moved.

The other amazing thing was Dad talking about Terri's daughter, Rachel. Rachel was expecting her second child in June 2008, so, of course, Dad could not have known she was pregnant when he passed away. Through Guisela, Dad told Terri he was sending a special soul for Rachel's baby. Hunter Matthew was born on June 5, and when Terri looks into his eyes, she sees Dad. More importantly, Hunter is the sweetest and happiest little boy and is a special soul.

There were many other things said during our visit with Guisela, too numerous to mention. They were things only we would have known and shared with Dad. Guisela never asked questions about our family; we did, however, confirm what she told us was correct. She told us Dad was thrilled that he could, once again, communicate with his girls; we felt the same way.

We plan to visit Guisela yearly to talk to Dad and are so grateful for the opportunity.

Sandi Falk and Terri Eis

I Believe

I remember seeing Guisela at the elementary school where, at the time, our daughters were in the third grade. They were off on a school camping trip for a couple of days. I was so happy to see that when my daughter Dana sat down on the bus she immediately had a friend to sit with her. As I glanced down the walkway and saw Guisela standing there, I gave her a wave, assuming she was just as nervous as I was about the girls going off on the trip so far from home. It so happened that the friend sitting with Dana was Guisela's daughter, Paola. They became fast friends and shared a room on the camping trip. Dana would later tell me how much fun she had with Paola and how all they did was laugh all the time, and that made her feel happy.

Eventually Guisela and I met when the girls would get together for play dates, and sometime after that Guisela revealed to me her gift. Guisela shared this with me when I spoke to her of my husband's father recently passing away. We arranged for a reading soon after. I wanted to believe. I'm a spiritual person, but everyone naturally has an inner skeptic.

I was amazed by the things that Guisela would tell me that related to my father-in-law and his family. I had always been fascinated by the ability to connect with people who have passed on. I was surprised. It is not every day that you run into someone who has this gift. We have had many interesting conversations since that time, most recently regarding the passing of my own father. It was a difficult time for us. Shortly after his passing, I wished to have some contact with him if I could, so I asked Guisela to do a reading for my mother and me to see if we could connect with him. The following is the story of our experience.

We scheduled an over-the-phone reading with Guisela because my mother and I live in New York and Guisela lives in Florida. I find it so remarkable that she is able to do this over the phone. We arranged a time when my mother and I were both available. We were excited and prepared to receive any word from my father. We recited prayers that were read to him while he was in the nursing home and lit a white candle with the intention of welcoming the spirits.

The day came for when the reading was scheduled, and Guisela started it with a question: "What does the letter F mean?" I knew the answer right away. It was my father's middle initial, F for Francis. She went on to tell us that his father, my grandfather, was there to meet him when he crossed over and that he had brought him a bouquet of flowers. Why flowers? One of my father's hobbies was planting flowers. He started doing this after he had retired many years ago and developed a beautiful garden on the side of the house where

I grew up. I was amazed when my father started doing this because I had never seen him do anything like that before.

The next thing that Guisela told us was that he liked the tie. The clothes we prepared for him to wear during the viewing at the funeral home included a tuxedo that he had bought when my parents renewed their wedding vows for their fiftieth anniversary. The tie was a special detail that would add to his well-dressed look. My father always wanted to look his best when he was going anywhere, and his funeral was no exception. We were so happy to hear that he liked that tie.

I asked Guisela, "What is he doing now?" wondering what exactly it was that they do over on the other side anyway. She explained to us that there is no real time on the other side like we have here. ,Guisela then told us that he was planting flowers and baking. I thought to myself, "Oh my God, you're kidding me." My father loved cooking and baking. His specialty was "bobka," Polish bread. There would be flour and pans flying around all over the kitchen, and he loved every minute of it. He always made sure that each one of his six children was given a cake. Even after we all got married and lived in different parts of the United States, he would mail them to us. My mother and I said, "That's him!"

Another thing that Guisela shared with us was that his legs were fine now and that he didn't need his cane to walk anymore. My father had had a lot of leg issues in the last months of his life, and he never liked having to use the cane: It was just another sign to him that he was getting old. We were so happy to hear that he had great legs now. He then said that he could wear his shoes now and that he liked them. During his last months, he couldn't wear shoes anymore because of the lack of circulation; his toes were discolored and painful.

He also sent a message directed to my mother, telling her to take care of her back. My mom always took such good care of my father and often put herself second. My father always knew this, and he wanted to make sure that she remembers to take care of herself.

Guisela then said, "I see feathers, a sign that the angels are near. Saint Michael, the angel of strength, is here." She said that we needed him now and in the future to get through this difficult time after losing my father. She then shared with us that my father was counting pennies. We started to laugh. My father was always counting his change and looking over the grocery bill before he left the checkout counter to make sure they got it right. He was always pinching his pennies and never bought anything he didn't feel was necessary. We found this funny, mostly because my mother had started to treat herself to some trinkets and shopping to lift her spirits. We were thinking, "He knows this and is trying to save money over here."

He also told us, through Guisela, that the clothes my mom was wearing were too dark. Again we laughed, because she was wearing something dark during the reading, and Guisela asked if it was brown. It was, as a matter of fact. She was wearing a dark brown jogging suit. Guisela told us that he didn't want anyone to wear dark colors and that my mother looks better in bright colors. All of the kids had been telling her the same thing right after my father passed away. We all wanted her to go out and buy herself some nice, bright, pretty clothes so that she would feel happy.

After that, Guisela told us that he was rocking a baby. This baby could only be my brother's first child. Her name was Alexandria. She had had heart complications and only lived for two weeks. At this point, my mother and I were so amazed that all of this information was coming through to us. Guisela then shared with us that she could hear a dog barking. I thought to myself, "I know exactly who that is." It was the little brown poodle that my father bought for me when I was young. It was a special gesture on his part to bring her into my life. She lived until she was sixteen, and I am so happy that she is with him now. My mother and I were overwhelmed, and we couldn't help but feel that Dad was in the room with us.

Guisela then told us that my father was standing in a circle with his parents and my mother's parents. My grandmother on my mother's side sent a message telling us that she loves my mother. In that message, she added that my mother had been stubborn when she was a young girl. We started to laugh again. Guisela then went on to say that my father wanted his oldest son not to feel bad that he didn't make it. We knew what he meant by this. Most of us had flown in from various parts of the state when he was in his final days. My oldest brother could not make it in time and flew in the next day. He wanted to relieve my brother of guilt and to send him a message of happiness.

He then told us, through Guisela, that he didn't want my sister to feel that she hadn't done enough for him. He told us to tell her not to feel bad, because she did everything she could do and more. My sister had taken my parents into her home when it became apparent that they would be better off living with family because my father's health was changing. After a few years, her life was changing also, and my parents had to make a move to another family member's home. She had always felt bad about this and wished she could've done more. But Dad had sent her a message of thanks.

My father went on to tell me not to cry, because that makes him sad. I said, "Dad, I will try to be as happy as I can here in this life," because I want him to be happy over there too. The last thing that my father said through Guisela was that he wants us all to know that he loves all his children equally. Our reading was amazing. I felt like my dad, not just Guisela, had been on the other line with us. We felt that he was talking directly to us. Guisela was his voice. There were so many personal things that my Dad would do and say, and it was so exciting to hear that he was actually conveying this to us.

I cherish Guisela's friendship. She is such a caring and genuine person, and I have been blessed by heaven to have her in my life. Thank you, Guisela. You are my angel and I love you. Thank you, Paola, for being the "little angel" that sat with Dana and in turn brought Guisela into my life.

My father was a man that had plenty of determination. He lived to be ninety and went through kidney dialysis during the last five years of his life. He went through many surgeries and struggles to make it to that age, and I used to call him the "Energizer bunny." The nurses that took care of him during dialysis called him "Superman." He was.

This is dedicated to my dad, Edward Kole. He knows I believe.

Janet Haugh

Introduction

I am just a simple person who wants to share her amazing stories and real-life experiences with you.

I believe that there are a lot of people out there who are like me and that they may need some help in understanding themselves and the signs that they may be receiving. Many people don't know that they are natural-born mediums. If you are one of them, I hope that this book helps you to realize that there is nothing wrong with your gift. I want to encourage you to develop your psychic abilities.

The gift can be confusing and frightening at the beginning. The unknown will always make you feel afraid until you understand its purpose.

Welcome your gift from heaven: learn to love it and enjoy it. It feels wonderful when you know that you are helping someone. The hugs, kisses, letters, cards, words of appreciation, smiles, and happy tears are priceless to me.

Life exists for a reason, and everybody has his or her purpose. Mine is to provide this helpful service.

I hope that you will learn much from the stories that I will share with you.

Part One

Realizing the Gift

Part One

Realizing the Gift

My name is Guisela. I am married and am the mother of three wonderful children, Paola (age twenty-one), Anthony (age twelve), and Christopher (age four). I'm currently working for a hospital in Florida that I've been at for a little over three years now, and I love it. Before I moved down here, I worked for another hospital in Long Island, New York, where I met some great people with whom I have shared astonishing experiences. I will be sharing some of these experiences with you later on, and it will help explain to you my growth not only as a medium but also as a person.

I enjoy my job because I provide services and help and because I am always around people. I love having the opportunity to meet and get to know new people. It goes hand in hand with my gift. My family and I moved to Florida about five years ago, and we bought our first house here. I also became pregnant with my third child in Florida. Christopher is a handful and is constantly keeping us all busy. I am a full-time mom and also have a full-time job, so I have a lot of responsibilities that give me a packed schedule: kids, home, spiritual readings, writing, and so on. I am thankful for my husband and my kids. Everything I do is possible because of them and, of course, possible with God's help. Without their help, this book wouldn't be here. Thank you.

I was raised by my loving mother, Betty, and my grandmother Isabel. My mother was a beautiful, strong, intelligent, and loving woman. My father and mother separated when I was two years old, but they were never legally divorced. My mother taught us to respect and love our dad even though they weren't together anymore, so we are still close to him. My mom was always an exceptionally hardworking woman. It was so difficult growing up seeing my mom struggle to put food on the table, but she always came through. We all learned a lot from her. My mother's main goal was to make her kids good, strong, happy people. Everything we are now is because of her. When she passed away, it was so hard for us to live without her. I think it's difficult to learn to live without someone you love, but we need to learn that they never forget about us and that they are always there for us, even if we are not able to see them. I feel so blessed to be able to communicate with her still because of this amazing and beautiful gift from God.

I am the middle child of three children, in between an older brother and a younger sister. My brother, Luis, and my sister, Elizabeth, have different personalities. I feel this makes all of our lives interesting, especially when we are together. My brother's personality is calm, but at the same time he is fun and has a great sense of humor. I enjoy talking to him because he is a good listener and a great believer. He's always interested in what I do (talking to those on the other side), and he shows me a lot of respect and support.

My sister is an extremely enthusiastic person and likes to talk a lot, as do I. We talk almost every day on the phone, and we also have a great relationship. My sister believes that our mom is always watching over her, and I think she believes in what I do, but I am almost sure she is afraid of the unknown. She can get nervous quickly, so I try not to push it on her. She has great respect for my opinions, as I do for hers. We all grew up together with my mother and grandmother, so we are all close and share a great bond. My mother was a believer who loved tarot card readings and the supernatural. Her best friend was a woman I called Aunt Sara, who was a great psychic and an amazing person. She was incredibly accurate and precise with her readings. She did a number of readings for me and taught me a lot about the mysteries of the tarot.

We all lived at my grandmother's house, and we all believed that it was haunted. We used to hear weird things, especially my mother and I. My grandmother never confided in me whether or not she was a believer, but perhaps she too was afraid of the unknown. Some people would say that ignorance is bliss. My mother, on the other hand, believed so strongly that the house was haunted that she never wanted to be left alone in it. She would wait outside the front door, sometimes for hours, until someone would come home. I remember she'd say that she would see spirits all the time and that it frightened her. I believe she herself was born with a powerful gift, but she didn't understand it.

Since the time I was small, I knew that I was different from the other children my age. Sometimes, while I'd be playing with my toys, I would hear a voice say, "Guisela, you are special, and God has special plans for you." I was around seven years old and didn't understand what was happening. I thought it was only a product of my imagination. It was confusing for me at times when certain things would happen—like I would see someone staring at me, then they would disappear in the blink of an eye. On many occasions I also had realistic dreams that would later come true. I used to think to myself, "What a coincidence." Now I know that there are no coincidences in life and that everything happens for a reason. Growing up, I was always afraid of what people would think of me, so I never shared my experiences with anyone.

I have always enjoyed the supernatural. At a young age, I enjoyed watching scary movies, mysteries, and cold cases. My mother, like most mothers, didn't think this was good for an eight-year-old, so she would catch me and turn my TV off. Although, as a child, I was encouraged to read by my teachers and my parents, I wasn't interested in reading. Not until I somehow came across a book titled *The Third Eye*. I couldn't put it down, and I finished reading it in two days. I thought to myself, "What an amazing book." Those two days I spent reading it changed my life forever. I felt as if I finally knew the path I had to follow.

That book was meant to be found and read by me. It definitely wasn't a coincidence.

During my teenage years, I tried doing the "normal" teen things, such as going out with my friends to try to have fun, but the voices and people from the other side were always there. I would try to ignore them at times, but they were always so persistent. When I was fourteen, I finally built up the courage and told my mother my secret, because I felt I needed help and someone I could trust to share my visions, dreams, and premonitions with. From that moment on, my mother became my confidant and assisted me in understanding things. She and I would talk every morning about my dreams from the previous night before I went off to school.

As my fifteenth birthday approached, my mother was planning a party for me. I was so excited and couldn't wait to have fun. Four weeks before the day, I had a vivid dream in which I saw my mother holding a black dress while I was trying on a beautiful pink dress. I was staring at myself so happily in the mirror, thinking about how beautiful the pink dress was, when suddenly my mother handed me the black dress she had been holding. She said, "This is the dress you are going to be wearing on your birthday." I couldn't believe it. She made me try the black dress on, and I put it on feeling incredibly sad. When I woke up the next morning, I was relieved that it had all been just a dream. Of course, I anxiously told my mother about it over breakfast. Around eight in the morning, somebody knocked loudly and urgently on our front door. We were scared but opened the door. To our surprise, my aunt was standing there, crying. She had come to tell us that my favorite uncle had died during the night. It dawned on me that this was the true meaning of my dream. Because of my uncle's death, my birthday party was cancelled and we all ended up having to wear black dresses.

Little by little, I began to understand the meanings of certain things. Now, after years of my premonition dreams, I have come to understand that when I see myself wearing all black it means someone close to me will pass. If I see myself and part of my outfit is black, it means someone who is not blood-related to me will pass. Through experience and time, I have learned to understand the clues the spirits, the angels, and my guides give me—but I must tell you, it wasn't easy.

Throughout my life, in dealing with my psychic abilities, I have seen many things that aren't in any sense "good." There are still many things that frighten me. That is one thing about the gift that you never get used to. Fear is a natural human reaction. The way that I deal with such things is just by believing that God is testing me to see if I can handle these new amazing experiences. I trust in him. We are all born psychic, and we all use the gift to communicate with the other side, although not everyone cultivates this powerful gift and uses it. I find that people are either not interested, afraid, or just so busy with the material world that they don't have time to think about these things. Sometimes people don't notice that they are ignoring something. Everyone experiences the gift differently, and although we are all psychic, not everyone is a medium or a profiler.

I remember a time when I was seventeen. My friend Marco and I were visiting my father at his house. While we were there watching TV, my father left because he needed something from the store, so Marco and I were alone. Marco got up during a commercial break to use the restroom, and he returned to tell me that he couldn't get in. Puzzled, he told me that the door was locked and the lights were on, as if there was already someone in there. I thought to myself that he must have made a mistake and reminded myself that we were alone in the house.

We walked to the bathroom to look together, but the lights were off and the door was unlocked. Marco looked me straight in the eyes and swore that he told me the truth about what he had seen. Of course, I did not doubt him. We walked into the bathroom together and stood right in front of the mirror—and, to our surprise, we both saw a man standing behind us in the reflection, staring back at us. Both of us ran out, incredibly frightened. Marco wanted to get out of the house as quickly as possible. He and I remain close friends, occasionally speaking to each other. To this day, he remembers about that night with the man in the bathroom.

A particular event that scared me growing up was something that happened when my brother's best friend came to visit us at our house. I'll refer to him as Charlie, although his real name is different. That particular evening, my brother wasn't home, so we asked Charlie to stay for dinner. After dinner, my mother and sister decided to go to my mother's room and watch some television. Charlie and I were in the living room talking and waiting for my brother to come home. Somehow we started sharing scary stories, and we were both enjoying the conversation. Suddenly, the front door blew open, and I felt a cool breeze come into the room. Then I couldn't see Charlie anymore. My eyes blurred, and I couldn't understand the rest of the conversation. I could hear Charlie screaming my name, and it felt like he was far away, but he was right in front of me. Panicking Charlie slapped me on the face and when I came to, I was able to see and hear clearly, again.

My mother and sister came into the living room because they had heard Charlie talking loudly almost to the point of yelling. When my mother frantically asked what was going on, neither of us had an answer. Charlie told my mother that the door had opened and that it had suddenly gotten cold. When he had turned to look at me, I had a different face on and wasn't talking anymore. Charlie told us that this had been the worst thing ever to happen to him. He was afraid and pale-looking. No one had an explanation for it. I never really understood what happened to me that day. I honestly believe that it was a wandering spirit who needed help from me, but at that inexperienced age, I didn't know how to help.

When spirits walk around, turning lights on and off or making noises, it usually means that they want to get your attention. Sometimes it is because they need your help. Because I am a medium and an open channel, I am able to see and feel them. That is why they come to me. Some of them need help in understanding that they don't belong in this world anymore. They need to understand that their world now is on the other side. On a lighter note, not all of my experiences were bad. I had wonderful, life-changing experiences as well, experiences that amazed me.

The first time I got married, I was young. My first husband was never into believing such things. He never talked about or believed in the supernatural before he met me. When I was pregnant with my first child, Paola, I spent a couple of weeks at the hospital because my daughter wanted to come into the world three months early. The doctors decided to have me stay in the hospital under close observation in case a problem developed. One of those nights, I was in bed and was in that state between sleeping and waking. That was when I saw this big, beautiful angel come into the room.

I thought he was unbelievably beautiful: his face, his smile, and the bright aura around him. The thing I remember most is the peace I felt when he walked through the door. I remember this as if it were yesterday. He held in his hand three envelopes. The first was small and white, the second large and white, and the third was also white but had red and blue stripes on it. The angel told me one was from my mother, one was from my sister, and the last was from my grandmother. During that time, my mother and sister were living in the U.S., my grandmother was in Lima, Peru, and I was in another state in Peru.

Just as the angel was going to hand me my mail, my ex-husband came into the room and the angel departed, carrying my mail. I looked at my ex-husband and said, "Did you see him? Did you see the angel?" He answered that he hadn't seen anyone in the room. I was sad that he hadn't seen the angel. It crossed my mind that he probably thought I was crazy in saying these things. I explained the vision to him, and he questioned me and asked me for details.

The next morning, I woke up thinking that I must have had a really weird dream, but all was revealed when my ex-husband showed up to see me. He had a strange look on his face when he came in, and he didn't even greet me. He asked me about the envelopes from my "dream" the previous night, and I described them to him again. He then reached into his pocket and handed me the same three envelopes that the angel had shown me. I asked how he had gotten them, and he told me that he had gone to our post office box earlier that morning and found them. Both of us were astonished. He asked me how I could have possibly known about the envelopes, and I told him that the angel had been ready to give them to me but that he had interrupted us. I was later released from the hospital. When my daughter, Paola, was born two months later another strange happening occurred, which I will detail in a later chapter.

Isn't it fantastic when you are thinking about someone and they call you or come visit you the next day? This happens to everyone, believe me. You might be thinking about a friend you haven't heard from in a long time, when suddenly your phone rings and there's your friend on the other line, the same person you were thinking of. Naturally, your first thought will be that it's a coincidence, but events like these happen because you were using your psychic abilities without even knowing it. It's easy to dismiss everything as a coincidence, but what is life if you can't explore its mysteries? Everything happens for a reason. In this case, you were calling your friend with your mind. Because we all have these psychic abilities, your friend was able to receive your message. That's why he or she called you. Psychic communication happens often, especially when people have a close relationship or bond.

Growing up, my brother Luis and I used to sing all the time, and my mom used to love it. I remember that when I was around sixteen or seventeen a great love song came out. The name of it in Spanish is "Bailemos," which translates into English as "Let's Dance." I loved that song so much. It was just so romantic, and every time the song was on I would start to sing along. I couldn't help myself. Like most teenagers, I was having problems with my parents.

My mother and I had a rough time getting along during my late teens and early twenties. I never wanted to talk much and had a bit of an attitude. One day, while I was doing my homework, the radio station played the song and I started to sing it loudly. I was living in the moment, feeling as if I were singing in front of a large audience. When the song ended, I walked into the kitchen and saw my mom crying. I thought she was upset and didn't like my singing, but when I asked what was wrong she answered that I had touched her on an emotional level with my singing. She had loved it, and that's why she was crying.

A few years later, when I was twenty-eight, I was still living in Peru while the rest of my family was already residing in the United States. Although I was the only one left in Peru, I wasn't truly alone because I was married and had my daughter, Paola. My mother called me for my birthday on July 18, sang "Happy Birthday" to me over the phone, and afterward began to cry. I asked her why she was crying, and she said that maybe this would be the last time that she would get to talk to me. Of course, I became upset and said, "Mom, next month you'll be back here for Paola's birthday, and we will all be here waiting for you." My mom would always visit us at least once a year in Peru.

After that conversation with my mother, I thought that maybe she was just sad because she missed me a lot, but what I didn't know was that she was sick. Nobody had told me anything, probably in an effort not to have me worry because I was so far away in another country. As my daughter's birthday got closer and closer, I started making plans because it would be an exciting time. I'd get to see my mom again, and we would all be together happily. As the days passed, I began to talk a lot about my mother to my friends and even to strangers. Then I began having strange dreams about her, until a few weeks later I received a call from my brother telling me that my mother was dying. I couldn't believe what I was hearing. It put me in such a state of shock that I felt as if I were having a nightmare. All I wanted was to wake up.

I didn't know my mother had leukemia. My family didn't mention anything to me because they didn't want me to worry, and they didn't think she would deteriorate so fast. They had been hoping that she would pull through. That night I cried my eyes out. By the next morning, I was getting everything ready to travel to Long Island, New York, to see my mother for the last time. That morning I asked my cousin Roxana to go to the store with me because I needed to get something for my daughter before leaving for the airport. While we were at the store waiting in line to pay, the radio suddenly began playing "Bailemos," which was my mom's song. At that moment I knew that my mother had died. I immediately told my cousin, and we rushed home so that I could call my brother. He confirmed what I already knew. My mother had let me know that she was already gone. That song had been the sign.

When I was in a lot of pain after my mother's death, I made the biggest mistake of my life: I became angry at God. I asked him why he had done this to me and why was he taking my mother from me. I was so angry that I told God that I would never believe in him again. I didn't want to believe in anything anymore because I felt betrayed. My mother was only fifty-one years old when she died. A few months after my mother died, I had a visitation from her. She looked so beautiful and healthy, and she told me that she was happy. She also told me that I needed to apologize to Our Lord for my behavior. She explained to me that it was nobody's fault, that it was her destiny to die when she did. Even now, I am still apologizing to God for my behavior during that time period.

God is not responsible for every bad thing that happens in this world. Things sometimes happen because they are meant to be that way, and sometimes people learn from hearing about the actions of others going through a bad situation. God is always testing us, and if you look around you can see how positive things can come from negative ones. I myself learned from the loss of a loved one to appreciate life a little more. Life is a learning experience. Since I've lost my mom, I always give people advice on how to treat others, our families, and our friends. Realize how important they are for you and how much you love them. It's okay—everyone forgets sometimes about what really matters in our busy lives—but love always exists. People can go so quickly, and you'll go on feeling as if you were too late. So always take some time to love.

I always think it's especially neat that my mother was the first one to know about my gift, because when she was alive she was my helper. Even now, in death, she is still my helper and my guide. I am lucky to have her.

I love you, Mom.

Part Two

Experiencing the Gift

Part Two

Experiencing the Gift

My gift wasn't a secret to my family anymore, but it was to everyone else—until I decided to open up to my closest friends, Gustavo and Jennifer. They really were great when they heard the news. They never once doubted me, and they always gave me the extra support I needed. Jennifer was my confidant for a long time, helping me understand my dreams, which strangely enough she was good at doing. The stories in which friends learned about my gift are incredible. In helping my friends cope with some of their difficult moments in life, they've helped me learn more about my gift and have helped me progress as a medium.

I remember one night when my friend Gustavo came to visit me. The entire time he was at my house he looked nervous and uncomfortable. I didn't know why he was acting so strangely. Suddenly, I heard some noises in my kitchen. I tried to ignore them. Then I heard some more noises coming from my room, and Gustavo heard them too. We couldn't ignore it any longer as we began to feel someone's presence. Gustavo became incredibly scared and said, "Guisela, something strange is going on here." At that moment he decided to leave, and when he stood up and started walking toward the door, I saw a young man walking next to him. I didn't say anything about it, only goodbye. I didn't want to frighten him any further. It was kind of amusing to me because Gustavo felt that by leaving the house he was getting rid of the spirit. What he didn't know was that this young man was leaving with him. The young man walking out with him was later revealed to be one of his family who was trying to communicate with him.

A few days later, Gustavo came back to visit me and talk about the other night's "little occurrences." I told him that I had seen a man walking with him when he was leaving and that this man was a family member with a message for him. The man had given me clues for Gustavo to understand who he was by showing me things he did when he was alive. Gustavo began to cry as I told him that I had seen a man who had died in a car accident and that he didn't want his cousin Gustavo to feel guilty for anything. He said it had been an accident. Gustavo revealed to me that his cousin had also been his roommate. While they were living together, he began acting differently toward Gustavo, and they had gotten into a few arguments. One night, after they had gotten into a fight, his cousin stormed out of the apartment angrily. That was the last time that they ever spoke to one another. Gustavo's cousin was involved in a terrible car accident, and he didn't make it. Gustavo had felt guilty for years and had blamed himself for his cousin's death. That was why he never told me about it. Through my vision, I was able to explain to Gustavo that his cousin's death was an accident, and not his fault. After that reading, I was so happy to have helped him and to see him smiling again.

Some skeptics don't want to believe that our loved ones are watching over us. They just want to make judgments about the people that do believe. Certain skeptics believe that what mediums and psychics do is evil and that it is only bad energy coming from the dark side. I can tell you that they are wrong. Mediums and psychics help people because it is our purpose to give hope. We were given our gifts solely to help people. We work with good energy, and we help skeptical people to be happy and to feel closer to God. It has been proven that there is life after death. My gift, has taught me a lot in life. I learned to understand people better and became a kinder person. Every reading and every day is a learning experience for me.

One day while I was at work, my mother introduced me to another woman—both were on the other side. I didn't know this woman, and I didn't know why my mother had brought her over to meet me. The woman was nice and kind, but I felt that she probably needed to contact her loved ones. I wasn't sure who she was related to, but they unexpectedly made me turn around and look at a woman coworker of mine who was behind me. This woman from the other side began giving me a lot of information as soon as I turned. She told me that she was my coworker's mother.

My coworker's name was Diane. I knew that Diane had lost her mom the previous year, but I didn't know her well, and we weren't close friends at the time. I thought to myself, "How am I supposed to tell Diane about this?" I paced nervously back and forth by Diane several times, until finally she started to notice. She looked at me with a curious expression until I finally decided to tell her. I said to her, "D, I want to tell you about my psychic abilities." I explained to her that I sometimes receive messages from the other side. The whole time, I was afraid that she would reject me or make fun of me, but she didn't. She was actually surprised but at the same time interested in what I had to say. Her mom gave me valuable information, and I was able to make this woman happy. She shared her reading experience with her older sister, who later came to me for a personal reading. But her father was skeptical about the whole thing and didn't believe.

Diane came into work the next day a bit upset that her father didn't want to acknowledge that his wife who had crossed over wanted to communicate with her loved ones.

She told me that her father had said that if I was genuine I should tell her what he used to call her when she was a baby. I told her that I didn't need to prove anything to her father—or to anyone else—and that if she or her father didn't want to believe, it was okay. I told her that the spirits don't like to be tested and neither do I. Diane agreed with me and turned around to go back to work. All of a sudden, I saw my mother holding out a single peanut in her hand. I turned and told Diane that her father used to call her "Peanut." She started jumping and laughing and said, "Oh my God, oh my God! That's what he used to call me! Oh my God, wait until I tell my dad!" I guess I didn't have to prove anything, because my mom proved it to them.

One of my greatest experiences with my mother is the story of how we found "hope." Years ago, my brother, Luis, was dating a woman that no one in my family liked. Everything started before my mother died. My mother had met her and told me that this woman wasn't right for my brother. She was different. My brother dated her for about two years, and during that time my mother died. My brother and I became distant from each other because of his girlfriend. We all knew that he wasn't happy. One night, I received a visitation from my mom. I saw myself waking up to go to the bathroom, and I saw my mother standing by the door. I said, "Hi, Mom. What are you doing here?" In her straightforward manner, she asked me what was I doing for my brother. Why wasn't I helping him? I told her that I couldn't help him because we weren't speaking to each other anymore. I asked her what she wanted me to do. I knew she was referring to my brother's love life, but I didn't know how to help—and, after all, he was an adult. She told me that I still had "esperanza," which is Spanish for hope. She started to leave, repeating the word esperanza until she was gone. Everything had felt so real.

That morning I went to work and took my morning break as usual. As I sat in the cafeteria with a coworker for a little snack, I told her about my dream, and we tried to figure it out together. I felt someone from another table watching me so I turned to look, and when I did I saw a woman sitting by herself at another table. I had never seen her before. I smiled at her and asked if she was new. She said that she had just started that week. I introduced myself and asked her what her name was. She replied "Esperanza," and I swear I almost fainted. My coworker kicked my leg under the table because we both knew what my dream had meant. My jaw almost hit the floor. It was hilarious. This was my mother's message.

A few days later my sister called to tell me that my brother had finally broken up with his girlfriend. It was obvious that the opportunity to introduce Esperanza to my brother came at the perfect time. So I set them up on a blind date. I knew that Esperanza was a good woman. She was a single mom who worked hard for her two kids. My brother is a good man who had been looking for the right woman for a long time with no luck. My mother had found the right person for him. All I needed to do was understand and trust her message and do my part. A few months later they got married. They have been happily married ever since.

Spirits always come to help. They are always there for you. You just need to acknowledge them and try to interpret their messages. Sometimes it is hard to understand what they are trying to tell you, but if you believe, have faith, and want to work with them you'll be able to get it. All you need is practice. The more you learn and know about the spiritual world, the easier it will be for you to understand them. They always come when you need them because that's their job. Believe it or not, they do their best to try to help their loved ones.

Spirits know how to reach us mediums. They don't care where we are, who we are talking to, or whether or not it's the right moment for us. As long as it's the right moment for them, it's okay for them to interfere, which can cause some interesting situations.

I remember a time when I was on a trip from Florida to Long Island, New York. While I was waiting in the airport for my flight, I noticed this older-looking woman who seemed unhappy. She was waiting to board the same flight that I was. It was around 7:00 p.m. when the airline announced that there was going to be a delay. This woman started to gripe right away and called someone on her phone just to complain about it to them. I heard her telling the person on the phone that she was not happy that night. I couldn't help but listen to her because she was standing nearby. I decided that I would stay away from her on the plane. Her attitude kind of scared me, and I thought it was better for me to stay away from trouble.

Twenty minutes later, the airline announced that the plane was going to be delayed another fifteen minutes. A different woman sitting nearby turned to me and asked, "Did I hear it right? Is there another delay?" I quietly answered yes. I didn't want the other woman to hear me, but to my dismay she heard me anyway and asked the same question loudly. I answered yes and smiled at her.

When she got off the phone, the woman decided to sit in front of me, so I concentrated on my writing. Suddenly, I saw a man standing next to her. I thought to myself, "Here we go again." The man I saw was a tall, older man. He asked me to tell the woman that he missed her and loved her very much. He told me that all he wanted was for her to be happy again and to see her smiling. I immediately said, "No way. You aren't making me do that." After that I asked who he was, and he told me that he was her husband. I didn't believe him. I thought he was playing games with me, because when I looked at her hands I saw she wore a wedding ring.

I asked him to go away, but he started to tell me that I had to trust him. I said that there was no way he could be her husband, because she was wearing a wedding ring. I also asked him to send me a sign that if I decided to talk to this woman everything would work out. At that moment, the woman reached into her purse and took a book out of it. When I looked at the book, I saw the title was *Believe in Angels*. I smiled because I had received my sign.

I looked at the woman and asked, "What are you reading?" She told me it was a book about angels that someone had given to her as a gift. She eagerly asked me what I was writing about. I explained that I was writing about angels, spirits, and the other side. She asked me if I had experienced anything spiritual before. Without any hesitation I said, "Yes, I am a medium, and I have something to tell you if you'll allow me to." I told her about the man that I could see standing next to her and what he had said earlier. The woman started to cry and told me that her husband had passed away three months previously and that it had been too hard for her to take the ring off of her finger. She wasn't a bad or angry person: she was just experiencing pain over the loss of her husband. The woman's attitude changed right away and she became happy after our conversation.

We boarded the plane and went our separate ways.

Part Three

Premonitions and Dreams

Premonitions and Dreams

Oftentimes, premonitions are shown to you in your dreams. A premonition can be something that you sense yourself, or it could be someone trying to tell you something. However, there are times when you might not quite understand the message. Dreams can sometimes be confusing and hard to remember. When the spirits talk to you through your dreams, it's like a puzzle, and you need to put the pieces together in order to interpret them.

In my dreams, when I see my teeth, it means someone is going to get sick or is already sick. When my teeth are falling out in little pieces, it means someone is going to die. When I see an engagement ring, it is the end of a relationship. Red or pink flowers mean love or friendship, white flowers mean an anniversary or new beginning, and yellow flowers can signify a birthday or happiness. I believe every medium or psychic is different. We all learn to understand the clues throughout the years and through our own personal experiences. It is best to share your dreams with someone you know and trust, because you just might end up with a "witness" later on.

On the night of September 6, 2001, I had a puzzling dream. I saw myself riding a bicycle around in a big city. I remember being totally confused while I was riding around, and I couldn't breathe because of all the smoke and dust in the air. I could feel dust in my throat and my eyes tearing. Suddenly, I saw three rows of people laid out in the middle of the street. There were other people walking around, stopping to look at each person individually to see if they recognized any of them. They might have been looking for someone in particular, but I wasn't sure. I continued riding my bicycle around the city, but I became so frightened that I said to myself, "I have to get out of here. Something is seriously wrong." I began to pedal faster and faster until I was out of that place.

When I woke up, I was bewildered because I didn't understand my situation in that dream at all. When I arrived at work that day, I told a coworker nicknamed Little Mike about my strange dream. He also thought the dream was strange and didn't know what to make of it. I like to share my dreams with people because, if something similar actually happens in real life, I have a witness to prove that I'm not just making up stories after the fact. The following week, on September 11, I was at work and noticed people gathering together. Nobody was working; everyone was rushing toward the cafeteria where there were TVs.

Little Mike came running toward me saying, "Guisela, do you remember your dream?"

"Which one?" I replied.

"The one where you were riding your bike and there were dead people lying in the middle of the street."

"Of course I remember."

"Your dream is happening right now," Little Mike told me.

We both ran to the cafeteria to see what was happening on the news. We witnessed the horrible tragedy of the planes flying into the Twin Towers and the loss of innocent lives. I was horrified and upset. I broke down in tears and felt guilty at the same time because I hadn't understood the meaning of my dream. I told some friends how I felt, and they told me that there was no way that I could have helped. Even if I had tried to help and had said something to the authorities, do you think that anyone would have believed me? The police probably would have thought that I was crazy.

Not long ago, I had a premonition in a dream with an upsetting outcome. I spoke to my friend Karen at work about the dream I had had the previous night. I told her that I saw myself inside an unfamiliar building and that a lot of people were there. They were all hiding because a man had come in and started shooting at everybody. In my dream, someone was shot and died, but I couldn't see who it was. Subsequently, I saw a large number of police outside trying to save us. It was such a frightening dream that I could feel that my heart rate was up and I was sweating profusely while sleeping. I don't remember the exact date, but I know that I had the dream on a Tuesday or Wednesday night. Later that week, on Friday night after work, I was watching the TV when they interrupted the program for a special news report concerning a shooting in a Cape Coral, Florida, child care center.

A man had walked into the center and shot his wife to death. Everyone else that was there hid in the other rooms until the police surrounded the center and arrested the man. I didn't remember my dream at the time and didn't make the connection until the following Monday, when Karen and the rest of my coworkers were talking about it. Personally, I don't like to get these kinds of premonitions in my dreams. I'd much rather deliver nice messages to people: messages with happy endings or messages with hope and love. I love having dreams that when they come true make people happy and joyful—like the next story that I will share with you.

I'll never forget the time I delivered good news to my great friend Mauricio. He is such a nice person and so easy to talk to because he is kind, and he's good at giving advice. We had worked together for a while and become good friends. He knew about my psychic abilities, as I shared many of my experiences with him. He loved and believed every story that I had to tell. Throughout our friendship, he had always seen me giving our mutual friends messages, but I had never done it for him and he never asked. One morning while we were at work, he said, "Guisela, for months now I've seen you telling people things about their loved ones, but you never tell me anything and I'm wondering why. Does no one on the other side care about me or have anything to say to me?"

I hadn't thought about it until he asked me. I realized that I had never delivered any messages to my good friend, and I didn't know why. I completely forgot about it afterward, though—remember, I have a normal "busy mom" life. The following Sunday night, after Mauricio had asked me why I never had any messages for him, I had a vivid dream. In this particular dream, I saw myself inside a house that didn't belong to me. I walked around and checked all of the rooms: the house was empty. There was one room that kept grabbing my attention. It looked like a baby's room. When I looked into the crib, there was a baby smiling right at me. The baby brought immense joy to me. As I began walking through the living room, I could see through the large windows that Mauricio and his wife, Sonia, were looking at the house from the outside. When I awoke the next morning, I heard a voice giving me a message for my friend. I was so excited to go to work that day. I couldn't wait to talk to Mauricio.

At that particular job, I used to go in early to work my overtime in the morning. I always took my first break around 7:00 a.m. My friends Jennifer and Gustavo were having coffee with me when Mauricio walked through the door. I yelled, "Hey, Mauricio, I have something to tell you." He looked at me with a wide-eyed expression and ran to clock in. When he came back, his face was glowing as he sat down by me. I told him about my dream, and I was able to describe his wife from head to toe, having never even seen a picture of her.

He was amazed at everything that I told him. When I finished, he told me that he and his wife had gone to see a house over the weekend because they were planning to buy one. The room where I had seen the crib was supposed to be their first baby's room. He laughed because he and his wife had been standing outside of the house scoping it out for a long while. My friend and his wife had been trying to have a baby for some time but with no luck. I was happy to tell him, "Mauricio, before the summer starts your wife will become pregnant." He was so happy for the rest of the day, and I hoped that the message I delivered was right. A few weeks later, he and his wife went on vacation, and when they came back she was pregnant! He received the news the day before the summer started. The spirits are there for all of us. We just need to wish to hear from them, like my friend did. It seems that since I did that reading for him, the spiritual world has opened up for him, because after that he started getting message after message.

There is another wonderful story about Mauricio that I would like to share. This story takes place at work again but at another time. Mauricio, my other friend Mike, and I were eating lunch when I asked Mauricio if he had in his house a picture of his father that wasn't hung up. He couldn't think of any picture that he had of his father, so I continued to give him more information to see if he might remember something. The picture itself was brown and white, taken in sepia. I asked him about something that smelled like the ocean in the picture. I could also smell fish and crab. Suddenly, I saw Mauricio's father with a fishing net full of fish and a single large crab. For whatever reason, he couldn't recall anything about it. Mike asked him to think hard about it, but he still couldn't remember anything.

The next morning, Mauricio came into work with a big smile on his face. He rushed up to Mike and me and asked us to go out to the parking lot with him to see something. He said that what we had to see was too big to bring inside. We walked to Mauricio's car, and when he opened the trunk we saw a large photograph taken in sepia of his father with a fishing net in his hand with some fishes and a single large crab in it. Mauricio said that he had been looking for a place to hang the picture but had forgotten about it. It seemed that his father hadn't forgotten.

People believe that because I am a medium, my life is easy and problem-free. I can assure you that my life is not any easier or better than anyone else's. I go through difficult situations and have my own problems. I have to make important life decisions, just like we all do. My life is indeed a bit different because I believe. I believe in God, angels, the Virgin Mary, saints, and energies. I also believe that they are always there for us. I have hope, and my job here is to help people's faith grow. I am also here to help people move on with their lives, to help them find closure, and sometimes to help remove guilt from their shoulders.

When I do my readings, I always tell people that it is not about religion. I try never to preach any religion. I believe that people need to respect everyone else's beliefs. I have done readings for people that don't believe in saints or the Virgin Mary, which is okay with me. For example, if I see a saint during the reading, I will just tell the person to acknowledge them and that they are only here to render service to us. If we need any help in our lives, they are always willing to do it. I also explain to the person that they don't need to begin believing in saints or praying to them. They do not need to change their beliefs. Always remember that saints are spirits from the light. They were alive once, and sometimes they come during my readings because I communicate with spirits, and that is what they are.

When I began feeling more comfortable with this wonderful gift, I started giving readings to my friends and their friends. It was fun and amazing for me. I couldn't believe that I was doing it. I amazed even myself every time. I used to ask myself, "How and where am I getting all of this information from?" Although I already knew the answer, I was skeptical myself, and I do think of myself as a normal human being.

One day I did a reading for my good friend Steve. We were talking, and I told him about my abilities. He felt comfortable with it and was all ears. We both belonged to different religions, but as I mentioned earlier this isn't about religion. This is about believing. I can prove to you that a better place does exist, unless you don't want to hear about it. I was happy that such wasn't the case for my friend. He is a good person and is open-minded. I started giving him a lot of information about his father, who had been deceased for a few years. He was happy with everything that I said, until I told him that his father was talking about a cross that had been placed in the top drawer of a white dresser. I asked him if he knew anything about it, and he answered that his family didn't own any crosses. I knew that what I had told him was true, but I didn't want to be too pushy about it. The information I was receiving was from his father. That was the last thing that I told him that day.

That night, Steve went to visit his mother and told her all about the reading. He was surprised that his mother seemed so interested in all that he had to say. He said that she even turned off the television so that she could pay attention to everything. When he got to the part about the cross, his mother revealed that she knew what I had been talking about. She said that, at her husband's funeral, the funeral directors had placed a cross on the casket and that she had taken it home. She explained that she had put it in the first drawer of her white dresser. She validated the last part of the information that I had given to Steve. Now, every time I see something for him, he loves to hear about it.

Part Four

Skeptics,
My Favorite People

Part Four

Skeptics, My Favorite People

When people come to me for a reading session, I immediately know whether or not this individual is a true believer or a skeptic who just wants to test me. I can feel their energy before they even come to me. My spiritual guides are always giving me clues and hints. It doesn't bother me that much anymore when people test me. I believe it makes me a much stronger and more confident person. It's an ongoing challenge, and I am always prepared for it. Usually the people that don't believe come to a session and won't say a word: they'll just listen without taking their eyes off of me.

During these sessions, it seems that before coming to me they have trained themselves not to recall or make any connection with the messages they are getting. Perhaps they didn't expect the reading to be so accurate, so shock suppresses their memories. The truth is, these people are looking for proof from the other side. Everyone has the right to believe or not to believe. I don't blame people for testing me, because there are a lot of fakes out there. However, people need to know that there are also real mediums and great psychics around too. Although there is a little more work involved in these kinds of readings, skeptics are my favorite people to do readings for. It gives me almost a sense of accomplishment to make a skeptic become a believer. Even if they don't want to remember anything at the time of the session, I always receive a phone call from them the next day to tell me that the reading was wonderful, accurate, and precise.

I have many stories to tell about skeptics. One of them is about my close friend Michael. Michael is a kind man with a great sense of humor. Every time we talk, we joke around a lot. I became closer friends with Michael and his wife, Lori, when they found out about my gift. All of my other friends already knew about it, but I was afraid to tell Mike because I had heard him in the past making some comments about famous mediums—and they weren't exactly nice. Finally, our mutual friends Steve, Mauricio, and Lorraine decided to open up to Mike. We all talked and picked a day when we would reveal to Mike the truth about his good friend Guisela. When the day came and we were eating lunch together, I bluntly asked him for his opinion about mediums, specifically the ones on television.

"You all know how I feel about that. They are all fake, and all they want is people's money. I don't believe in those kinds of things," he said.

We all looked at each other, smiling. I looked straight into his eyes and said, "What if I were to tell you that you have a medium right in front of you, talking to you right now?"

"Who... you? That's so funny. Are you kidding?" he laughed.

"She's not kidding. She is telling you the truth," Steve said.

Mike gave me a surprised look, and I felt at that moment that I needed to give him some proof. While I was talking to Mike, I could see an older man wearing a green coat, holding himself up with his cane. This gentleman gave me a lot of information, which I shared with my friend. One of the important things he shared with me was about a young man (whose name he also revealed to me) who was driving an old-fashioned red car and had been involved in a car accident. The gentleman said he was present at the time of the accident and had helped. That was why nothing worse had happened, because he had been watching over the man driving the car. He also said that he's still eating vanilla ice cream.

Of course, my friend Mike couldn't make any connection, and I'll tell you why at the end of this story. Anyway, lunch was over, and I couldn't understand why this man had come to me saying that he knew my friend and wanted me to deliver a message to him. I was upset because it was important for me to convince one of my best friends, and I hadn't. The next day was Saturday, and around 9:00 a.m. my phone started to ring. It was a bit early for someone to be calling me, but I answered and it was Mike. He sounded excited and wanted to talk to me about the reading I had done for him the day before. He said that when he went home he told his wife, Lori, all about it—and she couldn't believe what she was hearing. She became emotional, saying that the man with the green coat was her father (the green coat was his favorite one that he used to wear all the time). He was talking about her nephew's accident with his first car, which was a old-fashioned red sports car. She also made a connection to the vanilla ice cream because it was her father's favorite, and one of the bonding things he used to do with his daughters was taking them out for ice cream.

Sometimes the messages may not be for the person you are doing the reading for. Sometimes spirits use that particular person to deliver messages to their loved ones. You can get messages for other family members, for your friends, or sometimes even for people you are not friends with. Our people from the other side know what they are doing. They know that their messages will get to the right person. Spiritual meetings are open for all of them—for the ones who want to cross over—and they all are welcome. For them, it is a great opportunity to get in touch with others, and they take advantage of it.

In Mike's case, his father-in-law knew that Mike would share the experience with his wife, Lori, and that she would make the connection and understand the whole thing. This gentleman used Mike to get in touch with his daughter, and he did a great job. My friend became a believer that day, and now he and his wife are always open to receiving messages from heaven. Now he loves his experiences with the unknown, and he has witnessed some of the other readings that I did for his family and friends. He has become a great supporter of me and of what I do. He is not afraid to talk about it anymore, and he is also not afraid to share his ideas with others.

Speaking of skeptical people, my present husband was one for a long time, and it was hard to convince him. When I started dating Paul, I did not talk about my gift because I didn't want to scare him away, so I decided to keep my gift to myself for a little while. I tried my hardest not to talk about it when he was around. I thought that maybe one day he would be ready for it.

One afternoon, my friend Diane called my home. Paul was sitting close enough to me that he could hear our conversation. Suddenly, Diane asked me, "Did you tell Paul about your secret yet?" She sounded excited and said it loudly.

"No, not yet," I replied.

When I hung up the phone, Paul turned to me and asked, "What secret is your friend talking about?"

I got nervous and started to tell him most of it, but I left out some details because I noticed that he wasn't interested in really listening to what I was saying.

Finally, he said, "Guisela, I don't believe in ghosts, spirits, or anything. I really don't want to talk about it anymore."

After I revealed my abilities to him, I talked about it every chance that I could but never got any answers back from him. My feelings were hurt, and I decided to confront him. We got into an argument. He became angry and gave me an ultimatum. He told me that if I really wanted to continue with the relationship, I should quit. Quit my gift as if it were a job!

That afternoon we were arguing—and, while we were, I could see a man standing next to him, but I felt that I couldn't say anything. I was in a jam and trying to avoid more trouble. I wasn't even listening to Paul because this gentleman was so persistent and gave information in a rush. The man was tall and slim; he wore a gray suit with a hat. Part of his face appeared to be burned. He told me that he had three names: Frank, William, and Charles. I started getting anxious and didn't have any idea what the man wanted. I did not know him, so I figured that maybe Paul did. I was so frustrated with the whole situation that I decided to ask anyway. The man was obviously there for a reason, and I couldn't avoid him any longer. I told Paul all about it, describing the man and giving him the names. When I asked him if he knew the gentleman, I got a big no for an answer. After that, we dropped the subject.

The next morning, I went to work and told my friend Mauricio about the situation I was going through. His advice to me was, "Guisela, if Paul really loves you, he has to accept you the way that you are. If he doesn't, he is not the right guy for you." I took this advice to heart and knew that my friend was right. I knew I had to make a decision.

Suddenly, I could hear my mom's voice saying, "Gigi, go and talk to his mother and sister."

My response was, "Are you kidding me?" I couldn't believe that she wanted me to go over there and make his whole family think that I'm crazy. That was a definite no. I had made up my mind, but my persistent mother wasn't leaving me alone. She just kept repeating the same thing, over and over.

I went over to my friend again and told him what my mom was asking me to do. My friend just looked back at me and asked, "Do you really believe in what you do? Do you love what you do? Do you believe in yourself?"

I just smiled and said, "Yes, I do."

"Well, then, you know what to do," he replied.

After that, I couldn't stop thinking about it for the rest of the morning. Finally, I decided to call Denise (Paul's sister) and ask her if I could stop by after work. "Of course. You are always welcome," she responded politely. I thought that the easiest way for me would be to talk with just one of his family members and ask for some sort of advice or help. So at the end of my shift I went to Denise's house, but as I was pulling up to the house I saw Paul's mom's car parked right in front. I sat in my car for a moment thinking, "Oh my gosh, what I am going to do now? They're both here!" I think that my mom may have made that happen. Spirits always work that way. They get everything ready for you. They make things happen the way that they should.

Sitting in my car, I knew that I had to make a decision right at that moment. I could either go home or go inside Denise's house and face the situation. I decided to go into the house, where they were both waiting. I didn't know how to start the conversation. I was so nervous that my palms were sweating. I started the whole thing by saying, "Paul and I are having some problems." They answered politely that they were sorry to hear it. "I have something important to tell you about me, and it's also the reason why we are having problems," I continued. Paul's mother, Betty, and his sister Denise were sitting in the living room facing me, quietly waiting for me to say what I had to say.

This part is going to sound silly. I had no idea how to begin, so I chose the same thing that the little psychic kid in *The Sixth Sense* said: "I see dead people." I just threw it right at them. Immediately after that, I asked them to not think that I was crazy and said that I was ready to do a reading for them as proof that I wasn't bluffing. I was expecting them to laugh right in my face or make some sort of joke about it—but, surprisingly, they were amazed with my confession and wanted to hear more about it. I was so relieved. I felt much more comfortable talking about my gift and decided to start with my reading. While I was talking to them, I saw the same gentleman I had seen when I was arguing with Paul. I wondered why I was seeing him again and why he had appeared at that moment.

Suddenly, I could smell flowers and corn, and I visualized other vegetables and heard a church bell ringing. I shared my visions and what I was hearing with them. I described the man with the gray suit once again and asked them both, "Do you know anyone that fits his description?"

Betty gave me a kind smile, while Denise stared at me with wide eyes. Betty said, "Guisela, he is my father."

I was confused at that moment and thought to myself, "How could Paul not have recognized his grandfather's name?" So I asked Betty why Paul hadn't made the connection, and she answered that not everyone in her family knew that Grandpa had those three names. When he came from England to United States, he only kept William as his first name. In turn, Paul wouldn't have known about the full name. She then explained to me that the scar on his face was from when he was burned in a car accident. The corn, vegetables, and flower smell were because he had had a small farm in England, and after he moved to the U.S. he still enjoyed gardening all the time. The bell had been because when he was young it was his job to call everyone to church by ringing the bell. The gray suit was Grandpa's favorite outfit, and he would wear it while visiting close family. Denise even had a picture of Grandpa with Paul at five years of age, in which Grandpa was wearing that same outfit and Paul was trying on the suit coat and hat.

Grandpa's purpose was to make his grandchild a believer and help our relationship. The day I spoke to Betty and Denise, I proved to them all that I do communicate with the dead. My husband became a believer. Now he is a big help and supports me with my gift. He has gained a lot of respect for the spiritual world. Since that day, I became close with my in-laws. Spirits are always there for everybody: they try their best to help us and to make things better for us.

Skeptics are my favorite people to do readings for, and I will now share with you another great story to help explain why that is. This particular story makes me so proud of myself, as well as proud of my angels and spiritual guides. In December 2007, my family and I decided to go to Long Island, New York, to spend Christmas with our loved ones that live there. On Christmas night, after having dinner with my in-laws, we all went to Aunt Irene's house for dessert. She is my mother-in-law's sister. I thought that my family was huge, but my husband's is even bigger. That night— just like every year on Christmas—everyone was there. We were happy to see them all. I was happy to see Aunt Irene and Uncle Bob because they are great people, but I was especially glad to see Sally, Paul's cousin's wife. She and I had been close since the first time I met her, because she is spiritual and a great believer. I feel comfortable when she is around.

When I go to family reunions or I am in some kind of social situation, I try not to talk about my special abilities. I enjoy spending a normal day having fun. But something always comes up when the people I am spending time with know about what I do. When I went into the dining area with my husband to have some dessert, my mother-in-law and her husband, Guy, were already there. Paul's cousin Billy joined us in the dining room and said, "Oh, maybe Guisela can help me with this dream." I immediately thought, "Here we go again," because I knew he was skeptical, and I started to wonder why he wanted to talk to me about a dream. A few more family members started to walk into the room and were listening.

Anyway, I tried to help him with his dream, but I don't think that I helped much. When someone does not believe, it is increasingly difficult to help them understand, especially when you are in front of a whole bunch of people, feeling weird and embarrassed, and just want to disappear. Sally came into the room immediately because she knew how I was feeling and wanted to give me some support. Billy responded to all my questions with a no or an "I don't remember." When I mentioned something about him starting golfing, he dismissed it with, "Oh, you probably heard me talking about it before." I was not interested in convincing him or anybody else that night, because I knew that at that moment I wouldn't be able to accomplish anything, but I promised myself that when the time was right I would.

Billy always vacations in Florida, and when he does he stays with us for at least one night. On February 19, 2008, he came to spend the night at our house, just like he does every year. He arrived around dinner time, so we relaxed and all sat together around the table to catch up. After dinner we continued with our conversation, and Billy asked

74

me why his grandfather never came to visit him from the other side. I answered that maybe it was because he didn't believe, so he wasn't able to sense him. Suddenly, Grandpa appeared again, and I instantly thought, "Here is my opportunity." I looked at Billy and said, "Your grandfather is here." Billy smiled at me, but this time he seemed a bit more interested. I told him that, to help him believe, I would need to tell him something that the whole family didn't know about. I told him I needed to tell him something that was more personal, something that only he knew. While I was telling him this, I asked his grandfather for his help and explained that I wanted him to give me new information. I had been waiting for this moment for a long time and felt that this was my only chance to convince this skeptic. Luckily, Grandpa answered right away and gave me some great information.

Here is the conversation from that night:

GUISELA: Your skin has become dry, and you have recently been taking good care of it.

BILLY: Yes it has. I have been putting lotion on every night..

GUISELA: I know that Easter is a special occasion for a lot of people, but what is making this coming Easter more special for you? Your grandfather is talking about it.

BILLY: Oh! This Easter I am planning to take my wife, Lucy, to Italy as a birthday present.

GUISELA:	Billy, your grandfather is telling me that you are planning to get rosary beads. I know it is not common for a man to have one, but he said he knows you are planning to get one.
BILLY:	Yes, I was just recently thinking about it now that I am going to Italy.
GUISELA:	Now your grandfather is saying you are having some leg pain and you also need to make a dentist appointment because you are having dental problems.
BILLY:	Oh my gosh, I've been getting some leg pain lately, and he is right that I need to make a dentist appointment.

Billy was amazed with the information he was getting from the other side, but his grandfather just wanted to give validation that Billy had been wrong—Grandpa was around and was watching over him. Spirits are wonderful and just want to be acknowledged. Billy was amazed with everything that I told him. His face was full of light, and his energy became bright. This is only a piece of our talk. In reality, our conversation was much longer, and he was much more interested this time around. The following segment was an important part of the reading.

GUISELA:	A man is crossing over for you. He said that you know him and that he considered you his friend.
BILLY:	I don't know who this man could be.

GUISELA: This man is crossing over with a football in his hands and is talking about the Super Bowl. He recently passed away—perhaps last year, because he is new over there. That is the information he is giving me. He said that you know him.

BILLY: I know somebody who died around Thanksgiving last year, but why is he crossing over for me? We were just coworkers, but we always used to talk about football and the Super Bowl because we're football fanatics.

GUISELA: He said please do not feel guilty because you couldn't make it to his funeral. He understands and still likes you. He said family comes first. Can you please explain this to me?

BILLY: Oh my God, now I know. He died before Thanksgiving of a sudden heart attack. He was so young and full of life that it was a shock for everybody. I missed his funeral because I had already made previous plans with my family for Thanksgiving. I have been feeling guilty ever since.

GUISELA: That is why he is here today. He just wants to make you happy and take the guilt off of your shoulders.

Everything that I said to Billy that night was accurate. He was anxious to share his story with his wife, Lucy. He told me he would have to wait to tell her everything, though, because he didn't want to ruin the birthday surprise trip to Italy. After that he would tell her every detail about his new experience and how this reading had changed his mind that night, and how he became more aware,. I felt so proud of my gift and my people from the other side. They really do change lives.

One night, a woman called me to make an appointment for a reading. She was polite, but I was able to sense something strange while we were talking over the phone. Something made me think twice about whether or not to do a reading for her. The next day, that same woman called me to let me know that the day she had scheduled the reading for wasn't good for her. She had forgotten she had something else to do that day. So we agreed on another day, which of course was perfectly fine. Two days later the lady called me again.

When I saw her name in my caller ID, I knew something was not right. She asked me if she could come see me the day we had scheduled the first time she called. I replied, "I still have that day available." This time she also asked me if she could come with her husband. Of course I said yes. At that moment I couldn't help but ask her if she was a believer, and she nervously answered, "I am." She paused for a moment, then told me that her husband was extremely skeptical and that she was having some trouble believing. What she told me didn't make any sense to me, because either you are a believer or you aren't. In my heart I knew that something was not right.

The funny thing about this story is that, when I actually got to meet this couple, the husband turned out to be more open to everything that I said than she was. His wife was determined to say no to every single thing that I said. She had turned out to be the skeptical one. The husband was the one who validated every message and related things to their son, who had died recently. At the time it had been less than a year since his passing. This gentleman was honest in telling me right away that he was skeptical but that everything I had told them was right. He also became frustrated with his wife because she was giving me a hard time and because she didn't recall or relate the messages that he did. The woman cried a lot during the session, and I really did understand her pain. I told her that she was not ready for this and that she first needed to heal and find closure. She was asking me for the impossible. The last question she asked proved that she was only testing me. She asked me to tell her the only way her son would eat tuna fish. I couldn't believe it. I refused to answer her question and ended the reading by telling her that I don't like to be tested and neither do the spirits.

On their way out, the gentleman asked me who his guardian angel was. I was pleased to answer his question. This man turned out to be so open-minded and was a big help throughout the reading. I believe he changed his mind about the other side. In the end I was so glad that he had come with his wife to the reading. Sometimes, we mediums try our best to help people, but they are not ready. Sometimes they are in denial; no matter what you do or say, you cannot make them happy. I learned that from my own experience. Situations like these used to make me sad, but they don't anymore. I learned that we cannot always make everybody happy. We cannot change people if they don't want to open their hearts and accept the unknown.

Part Five

Out-of-Body Experiences

Out-of-Body Experiences

The first time that I had an out-of-body experience, it was absolutely unbelievable. It happened when I was giving birth to my daughter, Paola. As a first-time mom, I was in a lot of pain, but I didn't want to ask for any medication, which was silly of me. If it is available, why suffer? Anyway, while I was in this cold and bright room trying to listen to the nurses' advice and supportive comments, I felt like I was dying. Or perhaps I did, at least for a couple of minutes.

One of the nurses and the attendant doctor were my personal friends, and they tried their best to make me feel comfortable and safe. But I really did not want to hear them keep saying, "You are doing great, Guisela. Keep breathing. Keep pushing. The baby is almost out." Childbirth is definitely one of those times when you don't want to hear anything—I certainly didn't. The pain was terrible. During the birth, there was a moment when I began to feel numb and their voices seemed far away. I began to wonder what was happening. The nurse I was acquainted with kept saying, "Guisela, push again. You are doing great," while I was thinking, "What is she talking about? I'm not doing anything."

A few seconds later, I began to feel hot, like something behind me was burning my back. When I turned around to see what it was, I realized that I was on the ceiling and the bright white light behind me was what was making me hot. When I looked down, I saw myself lying still below while the doctor and nurses were becoming frantic. My first thoughts were, "What am I doing up here?" and "How can I be up here and down there at the same time?" At the time, I was pretty confused, but I was able to see everything that was happening around me. I remember looking at the frightened nurses, at my pale face and numb body, and at a baby trying to be born.

I had guessed that I was dead and that I needed to figure out what to do next. It was then that I heard the doctor yelling out to me that if I didn't keep pushing my baby could die. I panicked and looked toward my baby. I saw her trying so hard to come out that I realized she needed my help. Right away, I went back into my body for the last strong push, and she was finally born. My daughter was born, and I was born again. I still don't completely understand what happened that day. I do know that giving birth is a situation in which many women lose their lives or come close to it, but all I can say is that it hadn't been my time.

After my mom died, I didn't believe that she was gone, at least for the first couple of months. It felt like she was still around, and every day I found myself waiting for her phone call. I tried to continue my life and pretend that nothing had happened. I felt so numb at the time. I hadn't given myself any time to mourn because I was in denial. I used to wait for her calls every day, but I never received one. After a long time with no letters and no phone calls from my mom, it all sank in. It finally hit me that she was not there for me anymore.

I believe that everybody who loses a loved one feels that way at the beginning because it's so hard to understand that you won't be seeing that person anymore. Deep down you're still hoping that everything is only a dream and that, when you wake up, the person will still be there. As time went by, I began to feel depressed. I had many thoughts of sadness and was crying almost every day. I wasn't happy at all—and, believe me, I tried hard for many years to hide my sadness because I didn't want anybody to see my pain. I cried a lot over a period of nine years. I couldn't even enjoy Christmas anymore and didn't celebrate my birthdays. I just wanted to die and be with my mom.

One night, while I was asleep, I heard my grandma whispering to me and woke up. Or, rather, my soul woke up. I was so impressed and happy to see her again. I looked at her and said, "Hey, Mama Bel, what are you doing here?" She responded, "Please come with me, because somebody wants to talk to you."

Suddenly, we were both climbing up an imaginary ladder, but we were going really fast, like we were flying. When we got to the top, I felt great. There was a fresh smell and a peaceful sort of feeling. Picture yourself on a large, open, and clean white place that appears to be empty but isn't: a place where you don't need anything except for love. In this big place, my mother and other souls were waiting for me. I didn't pay much attention to the other souls at that moment because I was so excited to see my mom. They were all sitting around a big oval cherry wood table, with my grandma standing beside my mother. My mother was on one side of the table, while the rest were sitting on the other side together.

I looked at my mom and said, "Mommy, you're here! It is so nice to see you again." I burst into tears while I hugged and kissed her.

My mom said, "Yes, I am here, and the reason I had you come visit me is because I don't want you to cry anymore. I want you to see the way I live and who I am sharing my life with on this side. I've been watching you cry throughout all these years, and recently your thoughts of dying made me feel like I needed to do something to make you understand life after life."

That was when I looked around to say hello to all who were sitting at the table. I saw all of my mom's favorite family members: my aunt Angelica, my grandfather Oscar, my uncle Miguel, Mom's cousin Juan, and my uncle Hugo. Once I realized who they all were, I greeted each one with a lot of emotion, but I did not get to hug or kiss them. I only waived and acknowledged who they were. Nobody else said anything; they all just waived back at me. My mother was the only one who talked. After I acknowledged them all, I felt like I was having the time of my life, and I told my mother that I had decided to stay with them.

My mom's tone of voice changed greatly as she told me no. That was when she made me look down, way down to where my two beautiful kids, Paola (nine years old at the time) and Anthony (one year old at the time) were sleeping.

"Look at those kids. Do you recognize them?" she asked.

"Of course. Those are my kids."

"Okay, Guisela," she returned, "Do you want your kids to cry for you every day of their lives because you aren't there with them anymore? Do you want your kids to feel the pain of losing their mom? Do you love those kids?"

I suddenly understood the reasons why my mom had arranged this meeting. My mom wanted me to understand that she was happy on the other side, sharing a beautiful and peaceful life with her family, friends, and other souls. She wanted me to see that she was healthy and full of life again, without pain or problems. I realized that she didn't need me where she was, but my kids needed me where they were. She went straight to the point and sent me out of there, saying, "You don't belong here. You belong down there with your family. Please stop crying and wishing to die, because that makes me sad." Then she made me come back.

When I woke up the next morning, my husband at the time told me that I had been crying and talking to somebody in my sleep but that he hadn't wanted to wake me up because it seemed like an important dream. He was right. It had been special to me because I was able to be part of a wonderful and life-changing out-of-body experience. Since that day, I don't cry anymore like I used to. I understand that I had been selfish in thinking only about myself and my feelings. After that visitation, my mom became my spiritual guide and helper. I felt at peace knowing that she was in a better place. Throughout the years, I've been working with my mother by my side. She's the one that helps me during my readings.

We all have out-of-body experiences in our lives, usually more than once. But because we sometimes don't allow ourselves to believe, our skeptical minds keep us from recognizing an out-of-body experience that can be confused with a dream or nightmare. I always ask people if they have ever experienced a time in bed when they were half asleep and half awake, body completely relaxed. Imagine thated when, suddenly, there is a feeling of falling or flying, and it makes your body jump.

Why do you think you jump, even though your conscious mind knows that you are on your bed? Everybody tells me that it's because of nightmares or that they don't know why this happens. The explanation to this weird happening is that our bodies and souls are always connected with a sort of invisible umbilical cord. Your soul knows that when your body is relaxing is the perfect opportunity to fly away and go places, to see things before your material body does—but, no matter how far your soul goes, it will always come back.

Because you are not completely asleep, you'll feel like something different is happening, so you get scared and make your soul return to your body abruptly. That's why it makes you jump. How many times in your life have you gone to a place and felt like you had been there before? How many times have you met someone that looks so familiar that you think you know the person from somewhere else? Sometimes this happens even though you are sure that this is your first time visiting that place and that it's your first time meeting that person.

Physically you were never there, but spiritually you were. This is what we call déjà vu. We need to understand that we were souls before we came to this world, and we become souls again when we depart. That is why I always say that there is nothing to worry about or to be afraid of. In death we are only returning to our natural state in the cycle of life.

Part Six

My Psychic Kids

My Psychic Kids

When my daughter, Paola, was four years old she began to amaze me by telling me things that convinced me that she was psychic. My ex-husband used to be a policeman in Peru, and he spent a lot of time at work. My daughter and I were always upset about his schedule because sometimes he had to stay at the police department for two consecutive nights at a time before having a day off. One of those nights when he was at work, my daughter and I were alone and decided to lie down and watch a movie. During the movie, Paola jumped off the bed and said, "Mom, open the door. Daddy is here."

The door was big and heavy, and we always locked it when we were alone. She was too little at the time to unlock it on her own. I turned to her and said, "Remember, your father is going to stay at work tonight." But, just in case, I looked through the windows and opened the door. No one was there.

Then, a few minutes later, she stood up from the bed again and said, "Mommy, open the door. Daddy is here." I was ready to remind her again that her dad wasn't coming home, when I heard the doorbell ring. To my surprise, when I went and looked through the peephole, there was her father waiting to be let in.

My son Anthony has also shown me his psychic side from the time that he was young. He had an "imaginary" friend for years. This boy's name was Danny. When your child tells you about an imaginary friend, you should pay close attention. Every afternoon from the time that he was three years old, Anthony would close his bedroom door and play "alone" for hours. There were many times when I knocked and started to open the door that he would rush to the door because he didn't want me inside his room. I often asked him through the door if he was all right. I just wanted to know what he was doing. He would always say, "Please don't interrupt me. I am playing with my friend Danny." One day I asked him why I wasn't allowed in the room while he was playing with his friend. He told me that his friend was afraid of me and that every time I opened the door he would leave.

That night I started asking him questions about his friendship with Danny, and Anthony gave me unbelievable details about Danny and his family. Anthony told me that Danny had died in a car accident with his mother and father. He had been feeling lonely until he finally found a friend that could see him and play with him. Anthony gave me an entire description of Danny and his family. I had felt Danny's presence quite a few times, but he never allowed me to see him. My son played with his spirit friend until the age of seven, and Danny even came with us when we moved to Florida. He was gone a year after that. I'm sure that he moved on completely to where he belongs on the other side. We haven't heard from Danny since.

When people die unexpectedly of a heart attack or accident, or other reasons, they sometimes don't understand they are dead until somebody helps them see that they don't belong here any longer. Since they were surprised by death, they don't remember what happened. You can see an instance of this happening in my favorite movie, *The Sixth Sense*. Spirits often want to continue with their normal lives. The only problem is that no one can see them or talk to them, so they get emotionally hurt. They don't know that they are dead and need help. They need someone to make them understand that they don't belong here anymore and that they need to find the light so that they can rest.

I never expected to add my youngest son, Christopher, to this chapter. I started this book when he was two years old, and he never showed any signs of psychic abilities until recently. The first sign he showed us happened when he was three years old. One Saturday afternoon, I was scheduled to do a reading for a woman and her daughter at my house. I was trying to get organized for the reading, when I saw my son playing with his alphabet magnets on our refrigerator. He looked like he was busy. Even though he did not know how to spell any words, he was having fun and seemed to know what he was doing.

Anyway, his nap time came around, and his father tucked him in. I decided to read some angel cards for myself. When I was ready to sit down, something made me turn around and look at Christopher's alphabet letters on the refrigerator. To my surprise, there was a name spelled on the door, separated from the rest of the letters. The name on the refrigerator was Mike. I thought to myself, "Hmm, I wonder what this means." Because of my previous experiences with children and their psychic abilities, I tried to relate the name with the person for whom I was about to do the reading. The name surprised me, because my son didn't know how to spell, the name was written correctly, and it stood out from everything else on the refrigerator.

A little while later, Jackie and her daughter arrived. We sat down and starting talking. Everything was going well, and I decided to ask about the name, trusting my intuition. I asked if she knew someone with the name Mike or Michael. She said yes, with tears pooling in her eyes. As soon as I mentioned the name, a young man crossed over for her like he had been waiting for me to say it. He started saying how much he loved her and missed her too. He was revealed to be her son who had been killed a few years earlier.

Right at that moment I understood why Christopher had spelled the name on the door. Who made him do it? Who had helped my son with the spelling? Had he been communicating with Mike? Yes, indeed. I told Jackie and her daughter about what my son had spelled on the refrigerator door that day, and I showed it to them. Jackie was amazed and happy about the way her son had crossed over. She added that Michael had always loved kids and that was probably why he had talked to my son first. That was the final validation for her and for me. I learned something from Christopher that day.

Children, regardless of age, are able to communicate with people from the other side as if it were a normal everyday thing. Since they are new to this world, they don't have many memories from here yet. They still remember the other side, since that is where we all come from. If your children say that they talk to someone inside your house that you cannot see or perceive, ask questions and ask for names. Ask for details of what they look like, and you will be amazed. You can't confuse an imaginative child with a psychic child. As I mentioned before, we all come from the other side, and we return there when our time comes.

When we are dying, we also communicate with people that are already gone, because we are getting ready to depart. Those souls are preparing you for death and are assuring you that everything is going to be okay. People who are near death sometimes mention names of deceased family or friends. They are not hallucinating or remembering things: they can actually see their loved ones waiting for them.

Part Seven

Animals in the Afterlife

Animals in the Afterlife

Many people believe that when a pet dies it is the end of that animal forever. This is not true. Animals have souls too. They come from heaven, and at the end of their lives they go back to heaven. How many times have you heard a story in which a cat, dog, parrot, or other animal saved someone's life? Animals are able to sense when someone is close to death and can also sense catastrophic events before they happen. Animals all have a lot of intuition and are psychic. They are intelligent, and just because they don't speak to us in our language doesn't mean that they don't know what is going on in this world. It is fascinating to hear from them when I do my readings. They are amazing. Their information is as good as the information I get from other spirits. They can give specific details and send love to their owners here on earth anytime they want. Often, when I do a reading for a person who was close to his or her pet, it makes me happy to deliver the pet's innocent message from heaven. I will share with you the great experience I had the first time I saw a dog during a reading. It was a touching moment, not only for the dog's owner but also for me.

One Saturday afternoon a man named Hugh, who is a spiritual man and a great believer, sat down with me for a session. I had met this man at the hospital I used to work for in New York. He was referred to me by one of the many people whom I had done readings for at the hospital. He is a retired cop and someone I never thought would ask me for a reading. Anyway, during my reading, I was suddenly interrupted by a loud bark. I did not understand what was going on, since I had never experienced an animal's presence in my readings. I tried to ignore the bark and continue. I was constantly interrupted by barks, which made it difficult to concentrate. At first I thought it was just a dog from outside my house, even though I knew that none of my neighbors had one.

Suddenly, I saw this beautiful dog wagging her tail with happiness and excitement. That was when I realized that she was there for Hugh. I asked him if he had owned a female dog; he answered yes with a surprised look on his face. I described the dog and gave him some unbelievable information. To both our surprise, the dog was talking to us! This nice gentleman started getting emotional and told me how much he missed his dog. He had loved his dog immensely. She had been his companion for many years.

I told Hugh, "She is talking about how much she loves apples," which was strange for me to hear. He told me that he used to peel an apple for her every day and that she loved it. I said to him, "She is telling me about a certain day that you left her alone to go on your boat. She cried and looked at you through the window. She is telling me that you don't need to feel guilty about it anymore."

Hugh did, in fact, remember that day. He told me that he had always taken her with him on his boat but that on that day he had wanted to be alone. Just as he was walking toward his boat, he turned around and saw his dog, sad and whining through the window. Even after her death, he had felt guilty about leaving her behind that day. By the end of the reading his guilt had been lifted, and he felt peace in knowing that she was in a better place. We both learned that day that animals go to heaven too. Ever since that particular encounter, I have been able to sense loved pets.

Another time stands out when animals played an important role in delivering a special message. I was doing a reading for a woman, and while I was giving her information about her mom, who had crossed over to "speak" to her, I kept seeing birds on and around her. They were birds of different sizes and colors. I was curious about the birds, but I didn't mention them to her right away. I needed to find the right time to ask, so I waited for more clues to find out the reason for what I was seeing. Now that I have more experience with what I do, I try not to get too excited and reveal something hastily without knowing its meaning. I've learned to be patient in interpreting these messages that I am to deliver. Anyway, when the reading was coming to an end, I saw this woman's mom saying good-bye, and now she was the one surrounded by birds. They were standing on her shoulders, her forearms, and the palms of her hands. That was when I asked the spirit if she liked birds, and she told me that she still loves them and still has a bunch of them.

At that moment, I realized that it was important for her daughter to hear what her mom had said about the birds, so I decided to share the information with her. The woman started to cry and told me that she had been waiting for this validation. She told me that even though my reading was accurate, this was what she was waiting to hear. She explained how her mom used to love birds and had always kept many different kinds of birds. Now that she was older, she had started raising birds too. I learned from my own experience that no matter how simple the message sounds or looks, I always need to share it with the person I am doing the reading for. It might not be important to me, but it could potentially be important to whomever I am doing the reading for. I had to remind myself that a reading is not about me, it's about helping another person and their loved ones on the other side.

Part Eight

Photo provided by: Lorri Acott-Fowler

Be Grateful

Be Grateful

I always hear people complain about every single thing: about how nothing is ever good enough for them and nothing can ever make them happy. Some people just want everything to be easy for them. Every time we want to complain about how unhappy we are, about how life is so unfair or how we never have good luck, just recall those who are by far less fortunate than we are. Think about all of the poor children who have been diagnosed with cancer and are fighting for their lives with everything they've got. Think about the thousands of children suffering from disease and hunger and how many of them don't complain about the immense pain that they're feeling. Think about how people who were born without the gift of sight or the gift of speech can do well in life and how they too are happy to be here. You can learn to appreciate life by thinking about all that you have been blessed with. Be thankful for what you have. Life is short—we need to enjoy every minute of it.

Who said that life is easy? Life is difficult. But if everything was easy for everyone, there would be no reason to live: no challenges, no excitement, and nothing to fight for. A world without a reason to live would be boring. God is always willing to help us, but he also wants us to work for what we want. Even with all those little or big problems we go through, life is beautiful and amazing. Always be grateful for breathing, seeing, loving, and feeling. Don't only look for God when you feel trapped or when you are in trouble. Look for God every minute of every day, and always be thankful for everything he does for us. Discover the reason why you are here. There is always a reason to be around. Open your eyes and pay attention to your angels and your spiritual guides. See their signs, listen to their voices, and follow their guidance. They are there for you and with you; all you need to do is acknowledge them.

Spirits don't use their own voices to communicate because they don't have them anymore. Instead, they use your voice. That's why it's easy to get confused when you think that you are just talking to yourself. When you are about to make a decision, no matter how important it is, you will hear a voice inside your head giving you advice or telling you yes or no. You'll think that it's just yourself in your mind. So, of course, you won't listen to the voice. In the end you might make a mistake, and everything could go wrong. You will immediately think, "I knew it. I had this feeling. Something was telling me not to do it." That first voice you heard was your spiritual helpers. The next one was you second-guessing yourself.

Sometimes we feel that we are alone and that nobody cares about us. We feel that there's nobody up there listening to our prayers. It's easy to forget that God, the angels, and our spiritual guides are there for us, the same way that it's easy to forget about loved ones who are also there for us. There are times where we just can't help but feel alone. When I moved to Fort Myers, it was all so new to me—I didn't know anyone and hadn't made any friends yet. I was feeling lonely without my friends and extended family. I even missed having readings. One day, while I was driving to work, I was talking to God and said, "What is going on, my Lord? Have you forgotten about me? Don't you love me anymore?" When I stopped at a red light, my attention was caught by a billboard that was changing from one advertisement to another. It changed to "God Still Loves You." I had received my answer and proof that God was listening to me. I couldn't help but cry. I do understand that not everybody has knowledge of the spiritual world and how the spirits do things to help us in life. My job is to share what I already know. It is never too late to learn and improve your life.

In today's world, people have become caught up in trying to look beautiful and young. People are getting plastic surgery now more than ever. Even the media is encouraging this situation. Commercialism is pressuring more women into getting breast implants and having big, sexy lips. Men are not immune to this phenomenon either. More men are visiting salons to get their eyebrows waxed. Like the women, they are getting Botox injections and paying visits to the gym six or seven days a week. Everyone is trying so hard to look perfect. It seems to me we have forgotten that we all are God's perfect creation.

When you go out and meet new people, there is always somebody who is interested in knowing your age. If you are older than they are, they will feel better about themselves, and if you are younger but you look a little bit older for your age, it can make somebody's day. The new era is all about beauty, perfection, and youthful attractiveness. Today's society is putting a lot of pressure on people, and that's hurting us. We all need to start looking inside our hearts and souls. We need to find our inner beauty, because inner beauty is what you will be left with in the end. Inner beauty doesn't fade away, only external beauty does. I agree that we all need to look and feel good. I believe it is important, but it is not something that we should be obsessed about. Learn to live and be happy with your age and life's changes; adjust to them. Always try to feel young, beautiful, and smart from the inside out. Feel the love. Enjoy the gift that is waking up every morning.

Part Nine

Cleansing Your Mind, Body, and Aura

Part Nine

Cleansing Your Mind, Body, and Aura

Our bodies and minds work like computers. If you don't take care of your computer by giving it the right maintenance—for example, by deleting cookies and old files and by keeping away from unsecure websites—your computer will end up getting a virus, and your whole system could crash. The same thing happens with our minds, bodies, and auras. When you are around people who carry negative energy—the ones who are always complaining and aren't happy with their lives—you will immediately start feeling tired and unhappy too. You will feel like you have just gotten a virus. The reason why that happens is because our bodies are like sponges. We absorb energies that circle around us, whether they are good or bad. Bad energies are like viruses, and you need to learn how to get rid them.

Learning how to protect yourself is the key. We have to protect our bodies, minds, and auras every day of our lives. I can help you by sharing some tips on how to do this:

- Always keep your body clean because it works in sync with your mind. Clean body, fresh mind.

- Every morning, before you leave your house, talk to God, your angels, and your spiritual guides and ask them for protection. Even if you don't know who your guardian angel or guide is, that isn't a problem. They know who you are, and they will find a way to communicate with you and guide you.

- While you are asking them for protection, move your hands in a way that creates a barrier around your whole body, starting with your head and moving down to your toes. Now you are covering yourself with an imaginary circle of protection.

- Believe in what you are doing, and think about bringing peace, love, and faith into your life. Wish for a good beginning to your day.

- By putting all of your senses and concentration into these exercises, you'll be able to feel the celestial energy from the universe.

- The circle of protection won't allow bad energies to get to you. It will protect you for the rest of your day; it will make the day better and life easier. We all know that important things take time to happen. You might not be getting or feeling anything different at the beginning. Just remember that everything takes time and practice, and the more you practice the better you will get and the better you will feel.

- If you already know that some of your friends are not a good influence on you, if every time you are around them your energy gets cloudy, just grab your imaginary computer mouse and click to delete them from your life. Only keep good friends and good people around you.

- A good friend is one that is always there for you, during good times and bad. They are the ones that love and respect you and have a positive attitude in life.

- Focus on love, appreciate what you have, and be positive under any circumstances. Live your life in full, without looking back at the past. Look to the past only when you want to remember good experiences, people, and memories. Try to forget the things that make you feel sad, depressed, or angry, because this can create negative energy in you.

- Always remember that the past cannot be changed. The only thing that you can do is learn from your experiences and not make the same mistakes. If you follow these rules, your present living can get much better, your future will be bright, and you will be surrounded only by positive energy.

- Have faith that God and his helpers are always there to assist you.

Thanks to the Readers

I just want to thank you for taking the time to read my book. It took me almost two years to complete. At the beginning of my book-writing journey, I thought it wouldn't take too long to finish. I also thought that it would not be hard to write a book. The truth is that I was completely wrong. For the first two months, I struggled with finding the right words to put things together. I had so many stories to share but no idea where to begin.

I asked my good friend Kathy for help, and she did help for a little while until she moved up North. Even after she moved away, she tried hard to help me. But she had many of her own things to take care of, so I decided to lift some weight off of her shoulders. That was when my daughter took over.

That was when I realized that sharing these stories from my life was my true dream and one of my life's goals. After that realization, all of my memories came back to me, and I was able to write them down clearly and smoothly.

This project has been a big challenge and a terrific experience for me. This is a dream come true.

Always try your best to accomplish your goals; never give up. Everything is possible. With help from God, your angels, and your faith, you can make it happen.

Believe in yourself.
Just believe...

Made in the USA
Columbia, SC
10 April 2019